I Spy

Written by
Rob Waring and **Maurice Jamall**

Before You Read

to drop something

to follow

to ride

to take something

hat

ice cream

jeans

seat

secret plans

spy

sweater

quickly

wrong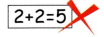

In the story

Yoon-Hee

Edgar

the woman spy

This is Edgar. Today he starts a new job. It is a very strange job. Edgar is a spy. He is in Washington D.C. in the USA. There are some papers on his table. They are secret plans. He wants to give them to a woman. She is a spy for another country. She will give him money for the plans. The phone rings. Edgar answers it.

I Spy

"Hello," Edgar says.

A woman says, "Do you have the plans?" She does not say hello.

Edgar replies, "Yes, I do. Did you buy a red bag?"

"Yes. I have your money," she says. "Meet me on the White House bus at ten o'clock. I'll put the money in the red bag. Do you understand?" she asks.

"Yes," he replies.

"But I don't know you," Edgar says.
"Don't worry," she replies. "I have long black hair. I'm wearing a green sweater, blue jeans and a gray hat."
"Okay. I'll sit behind you on the bus," Edgar says. "Put your bag under your seat. I'll take your bag. Then I'll give you my red bag with the plans."
"Okay," she says. "I'll see you on the ten o'clock bus. Goodbye."

I Spy 5

It is ten o'clock. Edgar is at the wrong bus stop. It is the Lincoln Memorial bus stop, not the White House bus stop! Edgar sees a girl there. The girl is wearing a gray hat. She has long black hair, and is wearing a green sweater and blue jeans. She is wearing the same clothes as the woman. She has the same bag, too. Her name is Yoon-Hee.

Edgar watches the girl. He thinks Yoon-Hee is the spy. He does not see the woman because he is at the wrong bus stop.
"Good, there she is. She's the woman on the phone," he thinks. "I'll get the bag and the money soon."
Yoon-Hee gets on the bus. Edgar follows her.
The woman sees Edgar with the red bag. She sees him looking at Yoon-Hee.

I Spy

"Oh no," she thinks. "That's the man with the plans. He's following the wrong person. He's getting on the wrong bus!"

She runs to the bus. She wants to stop Edgar from getting on the wrong bus. But he gets on the bus. He does not see the woman.

Yoon-Hee sits down and puts her bag under her seat.

Edgar gets on the bus and sits behind Yoon-Hee.
Edgar carefully takes Yoon-Hee's red bag. He puts his bag under her seat. Yoon-Hee now has the man's bag with the secret papers. Edgar thinks he has the money.
"Good," he thinks. "I have the money now."
The woman is looking at Edgar. She knows Edgar has the wrong bag!

I Spy 9

The bus stops and Edgar gets off. He looks in Yoon-Hee's bag. "Oh no!" he thinks. "There's no money! There's only an apple!" The woman comes to him. "You have the wrong bag!" she says. "I have the money here. That girl has the secret plans. Do something!"
"Oh no!!" he says. "The bus is leaving."

Edgar sees a man on a bike. He has an idea.
He pushes the man off the bike and takes it. "Sorry!" he says.
"Hey! That's *my* bike!" says the man. "Stop!" the man shouts.
Edgar follows the bus on the man's bike. The angry man runs after Edgar.

Edgar follows the bus. "I must get my bag back!" he thinks. He rides faster and faster and he is not riding carefully. He is not looking at the people in the park. He is only looking at the bus. Then he nearly hits a dog.

A man shouts, "Hey! My dogs! Look where you're going!"

"Sorry!" shouts Edgar. But he is only thinking about the bag. "Faster, faster!" he thinks.

Edgar does not see a woman with her ice cream.
He hits the woman and she drops her ice cream.
"Ouch!" she says. "Hey! My ice cream!"
She is angry with Edgar. "Stop! Come back!" she shouts.
But Edgar does not stop. He rides away quickly. He does not say he is sorry.

The bus stops at the Lincoln Memorial. Yoon-Hee and her friend get off the bus.

"Good. The girl's getting off the bus. I can get the bag now," he thinks. Edgar watches her.

"Wow, this is great!" says Yoon-Hee to her friend, Kerry.

"I want to take a picture," says Kerry.

"Yoon-Hee, go over there, please," says Kerry.

Yoon-Hee puts her bag down. "Okay. Smile!" says Kerry. Edgar sees Yoon-Hee's bag.
"There's my bag, I can get it now. I *must* get it now," he thinks.
Edgar goes behind Yoon-Hee. He does not want her to see him. He tries to get the bag.

Suddenly, a man runs at Edgar.
"My bike," he says. "Where is it? Give me back my bike!"
Edgar is very surprised and everybody looks at them. Kerry and Yoon-Hee see Edgar. He is trying to take the bag. Yoon-Hee takes her bag and runs to the bus.
The man says again, "Where's my bike? Give me my bike!"
Edgar is not listening. He is watching Yoon-Hee.

Yoon-Hee gets on the bus.
"Oh no!" he thinks. "She's going again!"
He pushes the man and runs to the bus, but the bus leaves.
He gets on the bike again and follows the bus.
"Hey!" says the man. "That's my bike!"

Edgar rides through the park again. He is riding faster now. He wants his bag with the secret papers.
The woman with the ice cream sees Edgar.
She shouts at him. "Hey you! Stop!" she says.
"Give me some money for the ice cream!" she shouts.

Edgar does not listen. "Stop!" she shouts again.
The woman tries to stop him. But she cannot. The bike is too fast. She drops her ice cream again. Now she is very angry. But Edgar does not stop. He does not say he is sorry about the ice cream.
"Come back!" she shouts. But he doesn't.
She is really angry with Edgar. But Edgar is not listening. He is only thinking about Yoon-Hee and his bag.

Edgar follows the bus through the park. He does not see the man with the dogs.
"Hey! It's you again!" says the man.
The bike nearly hits the dogs again. But Edgar does not stop and he does not say he is sorry. He rides away.
The man is very angry.

The bus stops at the museum. Edgar sees Yoon-Hee and Kerry get off the bus. Edgar gets off the bike. He watches Yoon-Hee go into the museum.
"Oh no! She's going into the museum! She has the secret papers," he thinks.
"What can I do? I must get the papers! I must stop her!"

Edgar runs at Yoon-Hee and tries to take the bag.
"That's my bag," says Edgar.
"No, it's *my* bag!" shouts Yoon-Hee. They are both pulling on the bag.
Kerry helps Yoon-Hee. "Hey! Hey! That's mine!" says Yoon-Hee.
"No, it's mine," says Edgar. "Give it back to me!"
Edgar and Yoon-Hee pull on the bag. The bag breaks and the secret papers go everywhere.

Suddenly, the men, the woman, and the dogs all arrive. They are all very angry with Edgar.
"He took my bike," says a man.
"Look at my dress! He did that!" says the woman.
The other man says, "He hit my dogs!"
"Get him!" they all shout and they all jump on Edgar.

Yoon-Hee looks at some of the papers.
"Look at this!" says Yoon-Hee. "These are secret papers."
"Let's tell the police!" says Kerry.
The police officers come. They take Edgar to the police station.
"Oh no!" thinks Edgar. "And this is my first day in my new job!"

Go Jimmy Go!

Written by
Rob Waring and **Maurice** Jamall

Before You Read

to catch someone

to win

finish line

lane

meter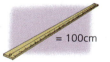

race

school principal

stadium

wheelchair

dangerous

second, first, third

slow

In the story

Jimmy

Anthony

Sarah

Mark

Mr. Williams

Mr. Roberts

"I'm in the 800 meter race," says a tall boy. His name is Anthony. He is writing his name on the notice.
"Which race are you in?" he asks a girl. Her name is Sarah.
"I'm in the 100 meter race, and the long jump," she says.
They are talking about Bayview High Sports Day. It is on Saturday. Everybody is excited about the races.

Go Jimmy Go!

Anthony's friend Jimmy comes to them. Jimmy is in a wheelchair. He loves sports very much.
"Hi, Jimmy," says Anthony. "How are you?"
"Great, thanks," says Jimmy. "Hi, Sarah," he says.
Sarah, Jimmy and Anthony talk about Sports Day.

"What are you doing on Sports Day, Sarah?" he asks her.
She says, "I'm in the long jump and the 100 meter race."
"Anthony, which race are you in?" Jimmy asks.
"I'm in the 800 meter race," Anthony replies.
Jimmy says, "I'm in that race, too."

Go Jimmy Go!

"Excuse me?" says Anthony. "Are you in the 800 meter race, Jimmy?" he asks.
"That's right. I am," replies Jimmy.
Anthony says, "Oh, but . . . but . . ." He is thinking about Jimmy and his wheelchair.
"What's wrong, Anthony?" asks Jimmy.
"Oh, umm . . . , nothing!" replies Anthony.

Sarah says, "You're in the 800 meter race. That's great, Jimmy. But be careful because Anthony's a good runner." Jimmy replies, "Yes, he's really good. I know. But I'm better than Anthony. I'm going to win."
Anthony is very surprised. He thinks, "Jimmy will never win. He's in a wheelchair!"

Go Jimmy Go!

Later, Anthony is talking to his friend, Mark. "Mark, did you hear about Jimmy?" Anthony asks. "Jimmy's in the 800 meter race! But he's in a wheelchair! He says he's going to win!"
"Yes, I know. Jimmy's always in the 800 meter race. Jimmy's very fast, Anthony," says Mark. "He's faster than me."
Anthony is very surprised. He says, "Excuse me? Jimmy's faster than you?"
Mark replies, "Yeah, he's faster than me over 800 meters!"

The sports teacher, Mr. Williams, hears Anthony and Mark talking about Jimmy and the race.
"Excuse me, Anthony. Did you say Jimmy's in the 800 meter race?" Mr. Williams asks.
"Yes, Mr. Williams," replies Anthony.
"Oh, I see," says Mr. Williams. "Thank you." Mr. Williams walks away.

Later, Mr. Williams talks to Jimmy.

"Jimmy, Anthony says you want to be in the 800 meter race. Is that right?" asks Mr. Williams.

Jimmy replies, "Yes, that's right. I'm going to win, too!"

"I'm sorry, but you can't be in the race," says Mr. Williams.

"Why not? I want to race. Anthony can be in the race. I can, too," says Jimmy.

Mr. Williams says, "I'm sorry, but you're in a wheelchair."

"But, Mr. Williams . . . ," says Jimmy. "I'm in a wheelchair, but I can still be in the race!"

Mr. Williams looks at Jimmy. "Your wheelchair may be dangerous to the other runners. It's too slow. You can help me start the races, or help with the . . ."

"But Mr. Williams, I *want* to race! I often race in my wheelchair," says Jimmy.

"I'm sorry, you can't be in the race," says Mr. Williams. "And don't ask again."

"But that's not fair!" says Jimmy.

Go Jimmy Go!

Later, Jimmy sees Mark and Sarah. He tells them about the race and Mr. Williams. Jimmy is angry with Mr. Williams.
"Mr. Williams says I can't be in the 800 meter race," he tells Mark.
"Really? That's strange," says Mark. "You often race in your wheelchair."
Sarah says, "Listen, Jimmy, maybe I have an idea. You must talk to Mr. Roberts, the principal."
"Yes, I will," he says.

Later, Jimmy goes to see Mr. Roberts and Mr. Williams. Jimmy says, "Mr. Williams says I can't be in the 800 meter race. Why can't I be in the race?" he asks.

"Well . . . ," Mr. Williams replies. "It's because you're in a wheelchair. And you won't win."

Mr. Roberts says, "Mr. Williams, Jimmy just wants to be in the same race with Anthony. He doesn't want to win."

"No, Mr. Roberts! I *will* win the race!" says Jimmy. The principal says, "That's okay. I understand. Jimmy wants to try, and that's good."

"But . . . but . . . it's dangerous," says Mr. Williams. "His wheelchair's dangerous for the other runners. There may be trouble. He may fall down and hit another runner."

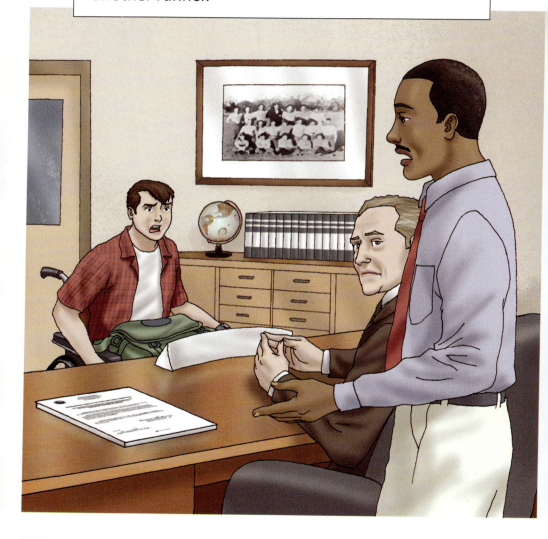

Mr. Roberts asks, "How many runners are there in the race, Mr. Williams?"
"There are six runners," he answers.
Mr. Roberts asks, "Can you make two lanes only for Jimmy?"
"Well, umm . . . Yes, I think so," says Mr. Williams.
"Good," says Mr. Roberts. "So Jimmy *can* be in the race," he says to Mr. Williams.
Jimmy smiles and says, "Thank you, Mr. Roberts." He is very happy now.

The next day, Jimmy meets his friends at the bus stop. They are going to school. Jimmy usually goes to school by bus with them.

"Come on, Jimmy. Let's get on the bus," says Sarah.

Jimmy replies, "No, thanks." He has a plan. "I'm not going to school by bus today. I'm going in my wheelchair. I must be strong for the race."

"Okay," says Sarah.

"I'll race you to school," says Jimmy.
"Ha, ha, that's funny, Jimmy," says Sarah. "See you at school."
It is very hard work but he tries and tries. He wants to be strong for the race.
"Come on, Jimmy," Sarah shouts from the bus.
Jimmy goes all the way to school in his wheelchair.

Go Jimmy Go!

The big day is here. It is Sports Day, today. Many people are at Bayview Sports Stadium. They are having a good time. Some people are getting ready for the races. Some people are racing.

Soon the 800 meter race will start. Jimmy is in his racing wheelchair. He looks very strong. He feels strong.

"Are you ready, Anthony?" asks Jimmy.

"Yes. I'm ready," says Anthony. "Umm . . . that's a great wheelchair, Jimmy!"
Jimmy says, "Thanks, Anthony. Good luck."
"You, too," says Anthony.
"I'll wait for you at the finish line," says Jimmy.
"No. I'll wait for *you*," says Anthony. He laughs.
They both want to win.

Go Jimmy Go!

Mr. Williams starts the race. Everybody watches them start. Jimmy starts slowly. His wheelchair is slow at the start. The runners are faster than Jimmy. Jimmy is last. But Jimmy is very strong. His wheelchair is going faster and faster, now.

Anthony is a very fast runner. He thinks, "I'm winning the race!"

Soon, Jimmy is going very fast. He's pushing his wheelchair very hard, but he is still last.

"Go, Jimmy. Go!" shouts Sarah.

"Yes. Go, Jimmy. Go!" he thinks. "I can win this race. I know I can! I can!"

Mark says, "Go, Anthony. Go! You're going to win!"

Jimmy hears Mark. "No, Anthony's not going to win," he thinks. "*I'm* going to win!"

Some racers are tired, they are running slowly. Jimmy catches them.

Go Jimmy Go!

Jimmy is going really fast now because he is strong. He is trying very hard. "Faster! Faster!" he thinks.
"Go, Jimmy. Go!" shouts Sarah.
Soon Jimmy catches more runners. He is in third place. He is getting nearer to Anthony.
"I'm catching Anthony," he thinks. "200 meters to go! I must win."
Anthony looks back at Jimmy behind him. He's a little worried. "Wow, Jimmy's fast! I must win! I can't be second! Go, Anthony. Go!" he thinks.

Jimmy is still in third place. He's going faster.
The other runners are very surprised by Jimmy.
Now he is second.
"Go, Jimmy. Go!" shouts Sarah. "You're going to
win, Jimmy! Go! Go!"
"I must win!" thinks Jimmy. "I must win!"
But Jimmy does not win the race. He comes second.
Anthony is the winner.

"Good job, Anthony!" says Jimmy.
Mr. Williams says, "Great race, Jimmy! You're very fast."
Jimmy replies, "Of course! I'm in this wheelchair every day. That's why I'm strong."
"Second place is very good, Jimmy!" says Sarah.
"But first place is better," he says. "I want to be first! Next year I will *win*!"

Do I Tell?

Written by
Rob Waring and **Maurice Jamall**

Before You Read

to break

to kick

to paint

to throw

bird

bottle

child (children)

garbage can

lake

park

seat

stone

ticket

scared

In the story

Ji-Sung

Scott

Mike

little girl

Ji-Sung is waiting at the bus stop. He is going to the park. He meets some boys from school, Scott and his friend, Mike.
"Hi, Ji-Sung," says Scott.
Ji-Sung says, "Oh, hi! What are you doing here?" he asks.
"Nothing much," says Mike. "Ji-Sung, where are you going?"

Do I Tell?

"I'm going to the park," says Ji-Sung.
"Good. We're going there, too," says Scott.
"Oh," says Ji-Sung. He asks, "What's that in your bag, Scott?"
Scott says, "Oh, this? It's paint."
"Paint? What are you going to paint?" asks Ji-Sung.
"Anything," says Scott.

"You're going to paint anything?" asks Ji-Sung. "I don't understand."
"Do you want to see?" asks Scott.
Ji-Sung does not understand, but he says, "Umm . . . , okay."
Scott looks around. Nobody is watching.
"Is it okay?" Scott asks Mike.
"Yeah, nobody's coming," says Mike. "Okay, do it!" he says.
Ji-Sung is thinking, "What are they going to do?"

Do I Tell? 5

Scott takes the paint. He paints the picture on the bus stop.
Ji-Sung shouts, "No, stop. Don't do that!"
Mike and Scott are laughing. "It's okay, it's only fun,"
Scott says. "Nobody can see us."
"But . . . ," says Ji-Sung. "It's wrong!"
"I don't care," says Scott. "It's really fun."

Mike says, "Can I try?"
"Okay," says Scott. He gives the paint to Mike.
He paints the same picture, too.
"Ji-Sung, do you want to try?" asks Scott.
"No way! I'm not going to do that!" he replies.
Scott says, "Hey! Quick! Somebody's coming!"

Do I Tell? 7

A police officer comes. "What are you boys doing?" asks the police officer.
"Who? Us?" says Scott. "We're waiting for a bus."
The police officer sees the paint. "Did you do this?" he asks Ji-Sung.
Ji-Sung says, "No. No, I didn't." Then the police officer looks at Mike and Scott.
"Did you two boys do this?" he asks Mike and Scott.
"Us? No!" says Scott. "We are *good* boys, officer!" says Mike.

Do I Tell?

"Be careful, boys," says the police officer. "Don't get into trouble, okay?"

"Of course," they say. "We won't get into trouble."

The police officer leaves. Scott and Mike start laughing.

"He didn't see us," says Mike.

Scott says, "Yeah, he can't do anything about it."

Ji-Sung says nothing. He thinks they are very bad.

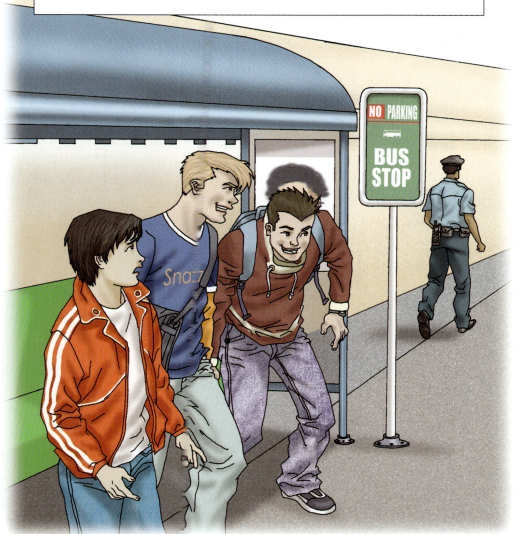

Do I Tell? 9

Soon, the bus comes. Scott and Mike get on the bus. Scott says to the bus driver, "One child ticket."
"A child ticket? You can't have a child ticket. How old are you?" asks the bus driver.
"I'm 10," says Scott.
"No, you're not! You're much older than 10!" says the driver. "You can't have a child's ticket."

"Okay! Okay!" says Scott. "Here's your money!" He is angry with the bus driver.
Mike is angry, too. He wants to buy a child's ticket, too.
Ji-Sung thinks, "Mike and Scott are very strange. I don't like them very much."
The boys sit down. Everybody looks at them.

Mike and Scott are sitting at the back of the bus. An old woman wants to sit down.
The woman looks at Mike, and says, "Can I sit there?"
Mike answers, "No, because I'm sitting here."
Everybody is very surprised because the old woman cannot sit down. The old woman says nothing. The people on the bus do not like Scott and Mike. They think they are very bad. Ji-Sung thinks so, too.

Ji-Sung gives his seat to the old woman. "You can sit here," he says.
The old woman says, "Thank you! That's very nice of you!"
Ji-Sung watches Mike and Scott. Mike gets a black pen. "What's he doing?" thinks Ji-Sung.
Mike writes on the back of the seat. Nobody sees him. Scott smiles at Mike.
Ji-Sung thinks, "Oh no!"

Do I Tell? 13

They get off the bus at the park. "Come on, Ji-Sung," says Scott.
Ji-Sung does not like Mike and Scott now. He thinks, "I don't want to be with them. I will get into trouble."
"No, thanks. It's okay," says Ji-Sung to Scott and Mike. "I'm just going home now."
"No. You're not going home. Come with us Ji-Sung. We want to show you a great game," says Scott.

He thinks, "I don't want to go, but Mike and Scott are bigger and stronger than me. I can't say no. What do I do now?"

"Okay, I'm coming," he says. But he does not want to follow them. They walk through the park. Some children are playing.

Suddenly, Mike kicks a garbage can. The garbage goes everywhere. He laughs. Some children look at them. They do not laugh. Then Scott finds some bottles.

"I have an idea," he says to Mike. Scott throws a bottle at another garbage can. The bottle breaks.
"Ha, ha, ha!" laughs Mike.
"I can do better than you," says Mike.
Scott gets some more bottles and gives one to Ji-Sung.
"Here, Ji-Sung, you try!"
"No, thanks," he says.
A little girl is watching him.

Mike throws his bottle and it breaks, too. The boys laugh again.

"This is fun, Mike," says Scott. They both laugh. The boys leave the broken bottles and they walk away. Ji-Sung is very sad. He is worried about Mike and Scott. He puts his bottle in the garbage can.

He thinks, "That was dangerous! It's wrong to do that. I don't want to be with them. I must tell the police, or I may get into trouble. I'm going home!"

Ji-Sung says to Mike and Scott, "Umm . . . , I'm going now."
"No, you're not!" says Scott. "I want to show you our new game. You'll like it!" he says.

Ji-Sung does not want to be with the boys. But he cannot say no to Mike and Scott. He is scared of them.

"Come with us," says Scott. Ji-Sung goes with them.

The boys walk to the lake. Mike gives some small stones to Scott and Ji-Sung
"Are you ready?" asks Scott.
Mike says excitedly, "Come on, Ji-Sung. You take some."
"What are you going to do?" asks Ji-Sung. He is worried about Mike's plan.

Do I Tell? 19

Suddenly, Mike and Scott throw the stones at the birds on the lake! Scott's stone nearly hits one of the birds. The birds fly away.
"What are you doing? Don't do that!" says Ji-Sung.
"It's okay, Ji-Sung," says Scott. "It's fun! Let's do it again."
Mike says, "You try, Ji-Sung."

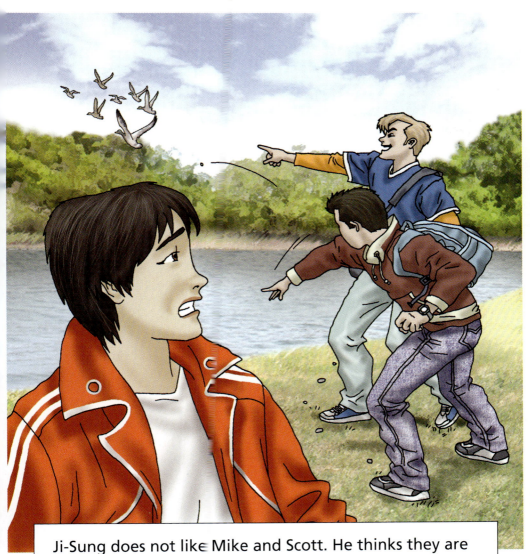

Ji-Sung does not like Mike and Scott. He thinks they are very bad. He wants to tell the police. But he thinks Scott and Mike will be angry with him. He wants to run away. "What do I do?" he thinks. "Do I tell? Or do I say nothing? Scott and Mike are big and strong. Maybe they will hit me!" he thinks.

Ji-Sung thinks, "Oh, what do I do? Do I tell the police?" He feels very bad.

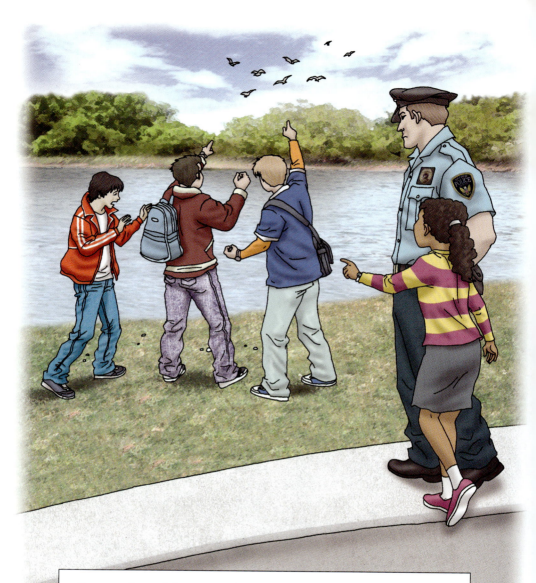

Soon, the girl comes back with a police officer. She tells the police officer about the garbage can, the bottles, and the birds. Mike and Scott cannot see the police officer. They are laughing at the birds. The police officer comes up to the boys.

"They are the bad boys," says the girl to the police officer.
The police officer says, "You three boys will come with me!"
"But I didn't do those things," says Ji-Sung.
"Is that right?" the police officer asks the little girl. "Did he do those things?"
"I . . . I . . . don't know," says the little girl. "I didn't see. But he was with the other boys."

Do I Tell? 23

"But I didn't do those things," says Ji-Sung.
"Maybe," says another police officer. "But you were with these other boys. And you didn't stop them. You didn't call the police. You're coming with us to the police station."
"Wait. Please listen," says Ji-Sung. "I'm sorry."
"Not now," says the police officer. "We'll ask your parents to come to the police station. You can tell us about it then."
"Oh no," thinks Ji-Sung. "What do I do, now?"

Lost at Sea

Written by
Rob Waring and **Maurice Jamall**

Before You Read

to dive

to paddle

to swim

anchor

engine

fire

island

marina

rope

shelter

stone

storm

wave

wind

wet

In the story

David

John

Faye

Tyler

Daniela

"Faye, please take this. It may rain later," says Faye's mother. "Yes, Mom," she says. Faye's mother gives her an umbrella. Faye, and her friend, Daniela are in Bayview Marina. They are going on their boat with their friends David, Tyler, and John. They are very excited because they all love to go to many islands in their boat. Today, they are going swimming.

Lost at Sea 3

"Do you have everything?" asks David's father.
David replies, "Yes, we have everything, Dad. Thanks. We have all the swimming things."
"And I have my new phone," says Faye. She shows it to her mother. "I can call you any time."
Faye's mother smiles, "That's great. Take care, and don't do anything dangerous, okay? Have a good time. Bye!"
"Okay, Mom," says Faye. "We'll be back at 4 o'clock."

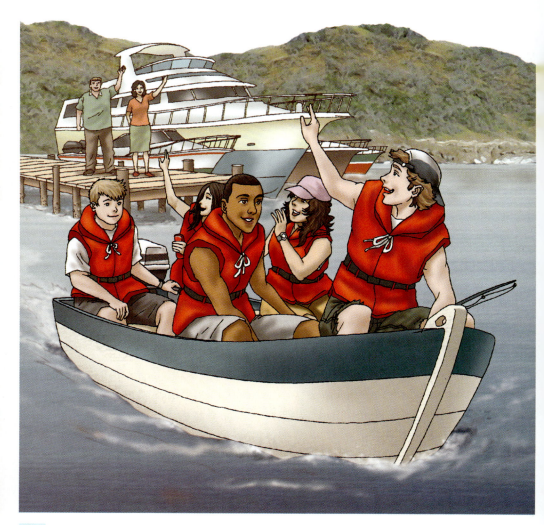

They leave Bayview Marina and take their boat out. They often go swimming. John, Faye, and David like to go diving.
"Let's swim here," says David. "This is a great place for diving. It looks fun."
"Okay," says Tyler. "John, put the anchor in, please," he asks.
"Okay," John replies. He puts the anchor into the water.

"Come on, John. Let's get in the water," says Faye. "It looks great!"

Faye and John dive down into the water. The boys swim around the boat and play in the water. They are good swimmers. Tyler tries to catch fish, and Daniela watches John and Faye. David goes into the water, too. They are all having a great time.

Later, Faye looks at her phone. She says, "I just had a call from my mother. She says a storm is coming. My mother wants us to go back."
"Oh really?" says John. "But I want to stay longer."
Tyler says, "But John, there's a storm coming. It's dangerous in this small boat in a storm. Let's go. David, please pull up the anchor and let's get back to the marina."
"Sure," David replies.

Lost at Sea

David tries to pull up the anchor. But it will not move. "Tyler! The anchor!" says David. "It won't come up. It won't move!"

Tyler says, "What? Oh no! I'll help you! John, can you help, too?"

John, Tyler and David all pull on the anchor, but the anchor does not move. They pull many times, but the anchor still does not move.

"What do we do, now?" asks David. "Think of something."
"Cut the rope," says Daniela. "We must get back. And the storm's coming."
Tyler cuts the anchor rope. Faye is looking at the storm coming towards them.
"It's getting darker. And the storm's coming fast," Faye says. "It's getting nearer, and nearer."
The wind is very strong. Then it starts to rain.

Lost at Sea 9

The rain and the wind are getting stronger, and the rain is getting heavier.

"I don't like this," says Daniela. "Let's go back. I want to go home."

David says, "Me, too!"

"It's okay," says John. "We'll be okay." But John is worried.

They are all worried. The rain is very heavy and they cannot see.

"Which way is the marina?" asks Faye.

"I don't know now. I can't see," answers Tyler.

Tyler starts the boat engine. He takes the boat back to the marina, but he cannot see very well. The rain is very heavy. It does not stop. Water is coming into the boat now. Everybody is getting more worried. The waves are pushing the small boat.

"I can't see," says Tyler. "The rain's too heavy. We'll never get back to the marina."

"Maybe it's this way!" says David. "I can see something. Let's go this way."

The small boat hits something very big in the water. Faye, John and Daniela fly out of the boat. They go into the water. David falls into the bags, and the bags fall into the water.

"Oh no! The bags!" says David. "Get the bags! Quick!" Everybody gets wet, but they are all okay.

They get back in the boat but they are very wet and cold now. "Is everybody okay?" asks Faye.
Daniela says, "Yes, I'm okay. But my leg isn't," she says.
Tyler says, "I'm okay. John looks okay, too."
"I'm okay. But look!" says David. "The bags are all wet."
"Oh no!" says Faye. "My bag!"

Lost at Sea

Faye looks into her bag. "Oh no! My phone's wet," says Faye. "It doesn't work! I can't call home."
Tyler says, "And the engine isn't working now. It's broken. It won't start."
"Oh no!" says Daniela. "What can we do?"
"There's only one thing to do," says Tyler. "We must paddle the boat to the marina. And let's paddle fast!"

They paddle for a long time in the wind and rain.
"Tyler, where are we?" asks Daniela. "I'm scared."
"Daniela, I don't know, I have no idea," replies Tyler.
"We may be lost."
It is starting to get dark and it is still raining. They are cold and wet. They are very tired. They cannot call for help.

The waves are pushing the small boat. They are in big trouble. John and David take the water out of the boat.
"Maybe we're going the wrong way," says Daniela.
Suddenly, John says, "Look, there's an island. Can you see it? Let's go to it."
They all paddle to the island. It is hard work. The wind is too strong, and the waves are very high. They paddle harder and harder.

After a long time, they get to the island. They get out of the boat. It is nearly dark, but it is not raining now.
"We were lucky to find the island. I'm happy we're off that boat!" says Daniela.
David asks, "Yeah, me too! But where are we?"
"I don't know," says John. "This may be Shark Island. Or it may be Bear Island. We were in the boat for a long time."
"What do we do now?" asks Daniela. "We can't call for help. Nobody knows we're here."

Lost at Sea 17

Faye has a plan. She tells her plan to the others. "It'll be dark soon. We stay here tonight," she says. "We need a shelter, some wood, a fire, some stones and some water. I'll make the shelter. Who wants to help?"

"I'll help to make the shelter, too," says Tyler.

David says, "Can I help you?"

John says, "I'll get some wood and I'll make the fire, and I'll get some stones."

Daniela says, "I'll get some water."

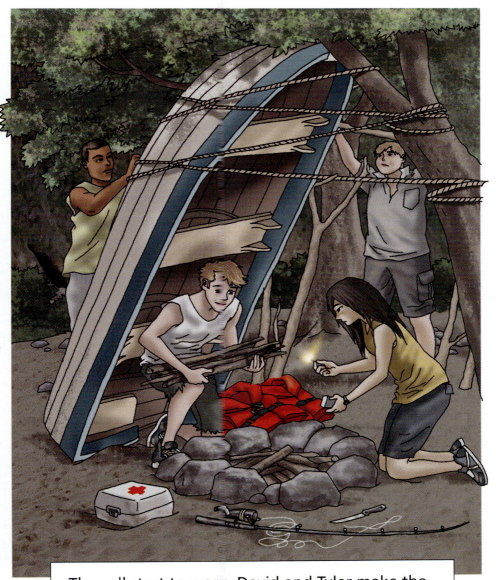

They all start to work. David and Tyler make the shelter with Faye. They work very hard.
"It's not good, but it'll be okay," says Tyler.
The shelter is not big but everybody can get in it.
"It's nearly dark. Be quick, everybody," says Faye.
Faye helps John make the fire.

Lost at Sea 19

Soon, the shelter is ready and there is a big fire. Daniela and David are getting some water.
"What are you doing, Daniela?" asks Tyler.
Daniela says, "We're getting some water so we can have it later."
"That's a good idea," Tyler says.

It's dark now and everybody is still cold. David says, "I'm still wet."
John says, "I can't sleep. I'm too cold."
"Come over here near the fire," says Faye.
"Let's sing some songs," says Daniela. "Does anybody know *Shining Star*?"
They all start singing and they feel better.

The next morning, they are cold and tired. They did not sleep well.
Daniela hears something. "Listen," she says. "What's that?"
"Look. It's the police helicopter!" shouts Tyler. They are all very happy to see the helicopter.
"We're here. We're here. Help! Help!" shouts David.
"Don't shout," says Faye. "They can't hear you!"
"Oh no! The helicopter is going away. Come back!" says Daniela. "What are we going to do?" she asks.

Lost at Sea

Faye says, "Everybody, get some stones! Help me put some stones here."

"Why, Faye?" asks John.

"There's no time. Get some stones, please. Big stones, not little ones. And be quick, everybody," she says.

John says, "But Faye . . . , why?"

"Now! Just do it!" she says. "Get some stones!" They run to get some stones. They write *SOS* with the stones.

Lost at Sea 23

Soon, the police helicopter comes back. Daniela shouts, "Help! Help!"
Faye's mother and David's father are in the police helicopter. They see everybody on the beach.
"They are coming for us," David says. "We're okay now!"
John says, "We're safe! We're safe!"
"What an adventure," says Tyler.
"But I don't want to do that again!" says Daniela. They all laugh.

Lost at Sea

The Shipwreck

Written by
Rob Waring and **Maurice Jamall**

Before You Read

to breathe

to die

to dive

to hear

to pull

to swim

air

anchor

dolphin

island

octopus

shark

treasure chest

water (sea)

In the story

David

John

Faye

Tyler

Daniela

John, Daniela, Faye, David and Tyler have a boat. They are all friends. Sometimes they go swimming, and sometimes they go fishing. Today, they are going to Shark Island by boat. They want to go diving and swimming.
Faye is looking at a notice. She says, "Are there any sharks at Shark Island?"
She is talking to her friend, John. He is sitting next to her.
"No, I don't think so," he says.
"Good," replies Faye. "I don't like sharks."

The Shipwreck

It is a very good day to go out in their boat. They take their boat out to sea. They stop near Shark Island. Faye puts the anchor in the water.

Daniela says, "This is a great place. This is going to be fun."

"Let's swim," says John. "Who's coming in the water? The water will be great!"

"I'm ready. I'm coming," answers David.

"Well, umm . . Not today, thanks. I'm not going in. I'll wait here," says Faye. "Maybe another day. The water looks too cold."
"I'll swim with you later," says Daniela.
David says to John, "Great! Let's look for some fish."
"Okay," replies John. "Let's look over there," he says.
John and David dive down into the water. They are strong swimmers.

David and John swim for a long time. They dive under the water. They see some beautiful fish. They look for some shells. "Wow! Look at these shells," thinks John. "It's so great here," thinks David. He is very excited. They are having a great time.

Faye looks in the water. She sees something. It's big and grey. "That's strange," she says.
"What's strange?" asks Daniela.
"There's something big in the water," she replies.
Daniela smiles and says, "Maybe it's David."
"Don't say that!" says Faye, but she laughs.

Then Faye sees something big in the water. "Look! What's that?" shouts Faye. Tyler sees it, too.
"Look out! John! John! There's a shark!" shouts Tyler.
"A shark!" John does not hear because he is swimming. He cannot see the shark.
"John! Come back, come back!" shouts Faye. She is very worried about John.
"John! John!" she shouts again.

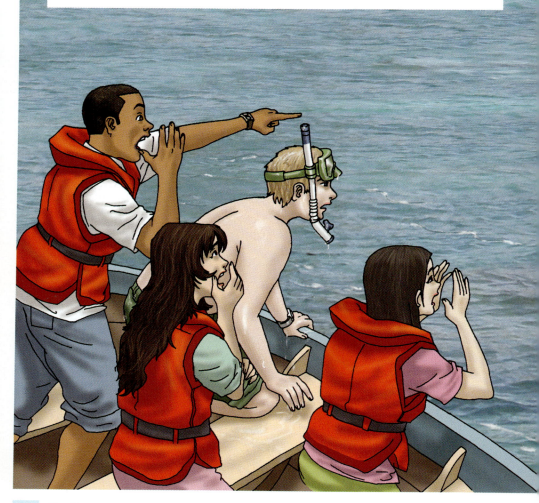

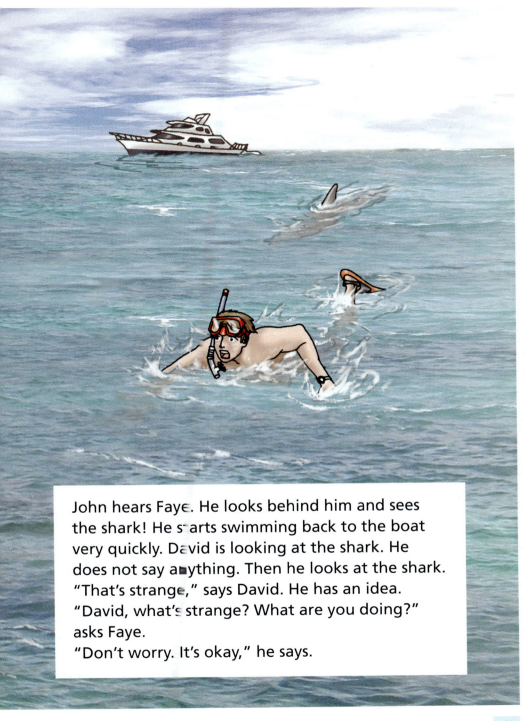

John hears Faye. He looks behind him and sees the shark! He starts swimming back to the boat very quickly. David is looking at the shark. He does not say anything. Then he looks at the shark. "That's strange," says David. He has an idea. "David, what's strange? What are you doing?" asks Faye.
"Don't worry. It's okay," he says.

The Shipwreck

Suddenly, David dives into the water. Faye is very shocked!
"No! David! There's a shark. Don't go!" shouts Faye.
"Stop!! It's dangerous!"
David does not listen. He swims out to sea. He swims to the shark. Everybody is really worried about David.
"What's he doing?" asks Tyler.

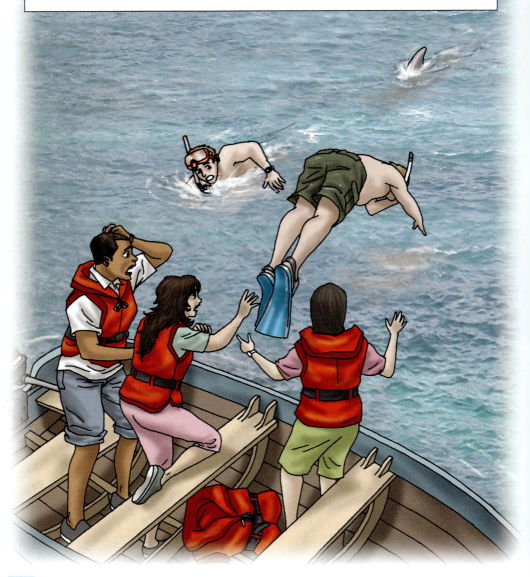

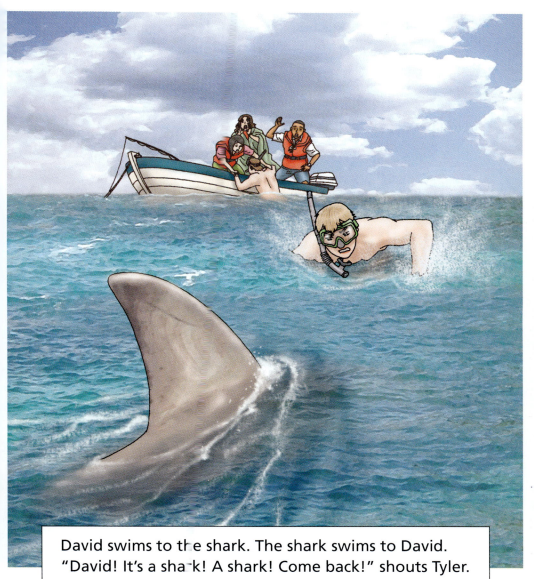

David swims to the shark. The shark swims to David.
"David! It's a shark! A shark! Come back!" shouts Tyler.
"You're swimming the wrong way!"
"Come back!!" calls Daniela.
David does not listen. He swims and swims. John gets to the boat. Faye helps him get into the boat.
"Are you okay?" asks Faye.
"Quick, get me in the boat," says John.

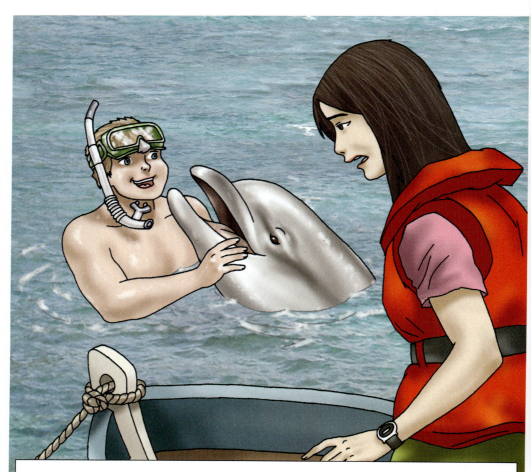

It is not a shark! It is a dolphin!
"Look at the dolphin," says David. "Isn't it great?" He swims with the dolphin to the boat.
"Oh, David! It's a dolphin!" says Faye. "You didn't tell us, David. Why? We were so worried."
"It's okay, Faye. Of course, I knew it was a dolphin! Sharks look different," says David.
Faye is angry with David. "But David, why didn't you tell us?" she asks.
David laughs and says, "Faye, you were really funny. You were so scared!"

"Faye, it wasn't a shark. It was a dolphin. You really scared me," says John angrily. "That was really bad of you. Never do that again, Faye," he says.

Faye says, "I'm sorry, John, but I was so worried. I didn't know it was a dolphin."

"It's okay," he says. "Be careful next time, please."

"Okay, I'm sorry," says Faye again.

"Come in the water, John. Faye, Daniela come in," says David happily. "Come and swim with the dolphins."

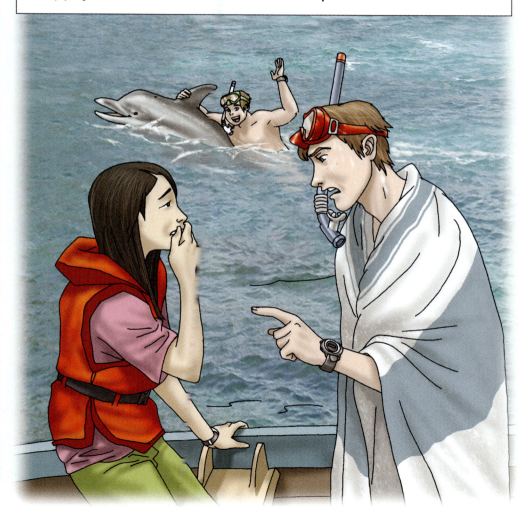

The Shipwreck

"Yeah, okay. I'll swim with them," says John.
Faye says, "Be careful!"
"Don't worry so much Faye! I'll be okay," says John. He dives into the water. David and John swim with the dolphins. Two more dolphins come to them.
"It's a family of dolphins!" John says.

John and David swim with the dolphins. They are having a great time. The dolphins pull the boys through the water. They jump high into the air. They dive under the water. Everybody watches them play. Tyler gives a small fish to a dolphin.
"Look at them, they are really great," says Daniela.
"Yes, they are," replies Faye.

The Shipwreck 15

John and David dive down under the water. John sees something. "What's that?" he thinks. He shows David and he understands.

"It's an old ship!" thinks David. They both swim to the old ship.

"It's an old shipwreck," thinks John. "Wow, I love this place," he thinks. The dolphins swim with them.

16 The Shipwreck

The dolphins take David and John down to see the ship.
The dolphins can swim very fast.
"This is great," thinks David. "I want to tell the others about this."
"Wow! This is so good!" thinks John.
They look at the old ship. There are some very old things. There are an old anchor, some old ropes, a lamp and many more things.

The Shipwreck

John swims to the back of the ship. He wants to look in it. He finds the name of the boat. It is *Lady Grey*.
"Wow, this ship is very old!" he thinks. "It's really great!"
The dolphin takes David back to get some more air.

John finds an old chest near the ship. It is a big old treasure chest. He shows it to David.
"Wow! What's in there?" he thinks. "There may be some treasure in it. Today is our lucky day!"
David and John want to look in the treasure chest. The dolphins take them down to it.

The Shipwreck

David and John push open the chest. There is a big octopus in the chest! David does not see the octopus. It takes his leg. "Oh no!" thinks David. "It has my leg. How am I going to get back to the boat?"

John and David hit the octopus, but it still has David's leg. It does not let him go.

John hits the octopus hard. But the octopus still has David's leg. He cannot move. David is in big trouble. John cannot help David because he has only a little air. The dolphins take John up to the boat. David cannot breathe. Nobody can help him.
"I'm going to die," he thinks. "I must get to the boat! I don't have much time."

The Shipwreck

David is in danger. He tries to get away from the octopus, but he cannot. Faye follows John down to help David. Suddenly, a dolphin hits the octopus. It is very surprised. It lets go of David's leg. Faye, John and the dolphins take David back to the boat.

Faye and John help David to get in the boat. They are all worried. David is okay now.

"David!" says Daniela. "David! Are you okay?"

Everybody is very worried about him. He is very tired. He cannot say anything.

"Will he be okay?" asks John.

"Yes, I think so," says Faye. "We must get him home."

The Shipwreck

Later, David feels better. David and John thank the dolphins for their help.

"David, you were very lucky. Do you feel okay now?" asks Daniela.

David replies, "No, not really. But I'll be okay soon, I think."

"That was great!" says John.

"Not for me!" says David. "But I want to come back!"

Mystery on the Island

Written by
Rob Waring and **Maurice Jamall**

Before You Read

to be sick

to sing a song

to take a picture

beach

camera

coat

forest

island

marina

pop music

secret

sound

video

In the story

Daniela

David

John

Faye

Tyler

woman

"Let's go in here," says Daniela. "Come on." Daniela, David and John are walking in Bayview. It is a great day in Bayview. It is Saturday morning and everybody is shopping. The friends are going to the music store. They want to buy some CDs.

Mystery on the Island

A big white car is going very fast. It nearly hits Daniela.
"Wow! That car nearly hit me!" says Daniela.
"Yes, I know. Are you okay, Daniela?" asks John.
She says, "Yes, I think so. Why's that car going so fast? Where's it going?"
"I don't know," says David, "But, maybe it's going to Bayview Marina, over there."

Later, when they are walking near the marina, David sees the car again.
"There's that car! It's near that big boat. Can you see it?" asks David.
John says, "Yes, I can."
"What are the men doing?" asks Daniela.
"I don't know. But I don't like it," answers David.
"Let's go and see," John says.

Mystery on the Island

They go to the car. They watch the men. They are big and strong. A man takes a woman out of the car. He takes her to the boat.
"Where's he taking that woman?" asks Daniela.
David says, "I think he's taking her onto the boat."

6   Mystery on the Island

A man comes to them. "Go away," he says. He is big and angry.
"Who's that woman?" asks David.
"Go away!" says the man again. "Go away!"
Everybody is very surprised and they walk away. The man goes back to the boat.
"Why's that man so angry? Why doesn't he want us to see the woman?" asks Daniela. "I don't like this. I think that woman is in trouble," says Daniela. "Let's tell the police."

Mystery on the Island

They all go to the police station.
Daniela talks to the police officer. She tells him about the car and the boat.
"Some men put a woman on a boat. We think they are taking her somewhere!" she says.
"I see," says the police officer. "Did you write down the car's number?" he asks.
"Umm . . . No," says David. "We didn't."
The police officer asks, "What was the name of the boat?"
"I didn't see it," says John.

"But they took the woman on to the boat," says David.
"We think she's in big trouble," says Daniela.
David asks, "Please come and look."
"Okay, let's go," says the police officer. "Where's the boat?" he asks.
"It's down at the marina," they say. "Please be quick!"
They all go to the marina in the police car.

But the boat is not there. The men and the big white car are not there. And the woman is not there.

"Where are they?" asks the police officer.

David says, "They're not here."

"Then I can't help you," says the police officer. "I think you're making trouble!"

"But the woman was here!" says Daniela.

"There's no boat and no woman here, now," says the police officer. "Don't make trouble!"

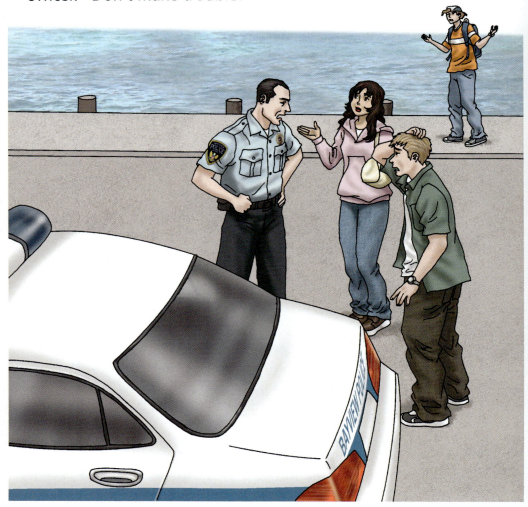

John, Daniela and David are angry with the police officer. They tell their friends, Faye and Tyler, about the woman.
"There was a man. And there was a woman in a long red coat. The man put her on a big boat," says Daniela.
"Where are the boat and woman, now?" asks Faye.
David says, "We don't know!"
"Let's go down to the marina and look for the boat. Maybe it will come back," says Faye.

Mystery on the Island 11

Later, they all go down to the marina. They see the big boat and the police officer. He is talking to the man from the boat. He is smiling.

"Look!" says John. "That's the police officer. He's talking to the man."

"Maybe the woman is okay," says David.

The big boat leaves. Daniela goes to the police officer. She talks to him.
"Is the woman okay?" asks Daniela.
"What woman?" asks the police officer.
John says, "The woman on the boat."
"What boat?" says the police officer. "Sorry, I don't know anything about a boat. I don't know anything about a woman. Now go away." They are all very surprised and they walk away.

Mystery on the Island

"I don't understand. That's very strange," says Daniela.
"Yes," says David. "He knows about the boat. And he was with the man from the boat. Then he says he doesn't know about the boat. Something's wrong!"
John says, "He's not telling us something."
"Why?" asks Faye. "Why's the police officer telling a lie?"
"Let's find out," says Tyler.
"Look, there's the boat," says John. "It's going to Shark Island. Quick. Let's go and look."

"How can we get there?" asks John.
"Let's go in *our* boat," says Daniela. "We must find her. We must help her."
They all get into their small boat. They follow the big boat to Shark Island.
"It's stopping over there," says Faye. "Let's go to another beach. I don't want them to see us," she says.
"Great idea," says Tyler. He takes the boat to a small beach.

On the beach, they hear something. "What's that sound?" asks John. "Can you hear it?"

"Yes, what is it?" asks Daniela. "Listen. The sound's coming from over there."

"But nobody lives on this island," says Faye.

Soon, they hear the sound again. "What's that sound?" John asks.

"Let's go and see," says Daniela. "This way," she says.

They walk through the forest. They do not want anybody to see them. They are following the sound. They are all very excited. Suddenly, Faye sees a big house.
"Look, there's a big old house," says Faye. "The sound may be coming from there. The woman may be there, too," she says.
"But nobody lives in that house," says Daniela. "It looks too old."

Mystery on the Island

They go nearer the house. "No," says John. "There are some men and their dogs, can you see them?"
"Look! It's the man from the marina!" Faye says.
"What are they doing?" asks John.
"I don't know," says Tyler. "Let's go and see," he says.
"No, it's too dangerous. I don't like this place," says Daniela. "The men look big and strong and there are many big dogs. I don't care. I'm scared. I'm going home."

Mystery on the Island

Suddenly, the man sees them. "What are *you* doing here?" he asks angrily.
David shows the man his camera. "We were taking pictures and we heard a big sound."
"No pictures! Come with us," the man says angrily.
Faye wants to know about the sound. "What was that sound?" she asks.
"Where are we going?" says Tyler. "Who are you?"
"Don't ask!" says the man. He takes them to the big house.

Mystery on the Island 19

"Look! There's the woman from the boat!" says Daniela. "She *is* here!"

Tyler says, "Wow! It's Patti Sanders, the pop singer!"

"Patti Sanders!" says Daniela. "I love her music! I sing her songs all the time! What's she doing here?" she asks the man.

The man says, "She's making a music video."

"Oh, I see! So the sound was her music!" says Daniela.

"Yes, that's right," says the man. "We want to make the video, but we don't want people here. It's too much trouble," he says. "We want it to be a secret."
"Look, there's the police officer!" says John.
Faye says, "So the police officer knows you're here, too. He knows you're making a secret video."
"Yes, that's right! He's helping us," says the man. "Do you want to meet Patti?" he asks.
"Of course!!" says Daniela.

Mystery on the Island 21

"Hello, I'm Patti," she says.
Daniela says, "Hello, I'm Daniela. I'm very happy to meet you. I know all your songs. I love them."
"Thank you," says Patti.
Daniela is so excited. "I love singing your songs," she says.
"Yes, she's a good singer," says Faye.
"Yes, very very good," says John. "She sings your songs all the time."

Mystery on the Island

"Really?" says Patti. "One of my singers is sick. She can't sing today."
"Oh, no," says Daniela. "And I wanted to watch you sing."
Patti asks, "Daniela, do you know my new song *Shining Star*?"
"Yes," replies Daniela. "I sing it all the time."
"I need somebody to help me. Do you want to sing it with me?" asks Patti.
"Now? Here? On video? Oh, yes please! Yes, please! Yes, please!!" shouts Daniela. She is very excited.

Daniela is singing with Patti up on stage. Her friends are sitting watching them.
"*You're my shining star . . . ,*" sings Daniela.
Patti is smiling at Daniela. Everybody is watching them sing.
"Daniela's a good singer," says Faye.
"Yes, very good," says John. "And today she's a star, too."